W9-CDN-633

Row Row Row Your Boat

ROW ROW ROW YOUR BOAT

AS TOLD AND ILLUSTRATED BY
IZA TRAPANI

Gareth Stevens Publishing
A WORLD ALMANAC EDUCATION GROUP COMPANY

J782.42164
Trapani

For a free color catalog describing Gareth Stevens' list of high-quality books and multimedia programs, call 1-800-542-2595 (USA) or 1-800-461-9120 (Canada). Gareth Stevens Publishing's Fax: (414) 225-0377.

Library of Congress Cataloging-in-Publication Data available upon request from publisher. Fax (414) 225-0377 for the attention of the Publishing Records Department.

ISBN 0-8368-2668-X

This edition first published in 2000 by
Gareth Stevens Publishing
A World Almanac Education Group Company
1555 North RiverCenter Drive, Suite 201
Milwaukee, WI 53212 USA

Original © 1999 by Iza Trapani. Original edition published by Charlesbridge Publishing, 85 Main Street, Watertown, MA 02472.

All rights to this edition reserved to Gareth Stevens, Inc. No part of this book may be reproduced, stored in a retrieval system, or transmitted in any form or by any means, electronic, mechanical, photocopying, recording, or otherwise without the prior written permission of the publisher except for the inclusion of brief quotations in an acknowledged review.

Printed in the United States of America

1 2 3 4 5 6 7 8 9 04 03 02 01 00

MLK
R0093094488

For Pat and Margaret,
Johnny, Daniel, Helen, and Anna,
May you share many merry adventures!

Row row row your boat
Gently down the stream
Merrily, merrily, merrily, merrily,
Life is but a dream.

Row row row your boat
Happy as can be
Sunshine glowing, off and rowing
With your family.

Row row row your boat
Stroke and follow through

Fumbling, flailing, oars go sailing—
What a clumsy crew!

Row row row your boat
Row with all your might

Rocking, bashing, water splashing
Better hold on tight!

Row row row your boat
Look ahead to find

Beavers damming, logging, jamming
Left you in a bind!

Row row row your boat
Stop to have a munch
Chomping, snacking, slurping, smacking
What a noisy bunch!

Row row row your boat
Better row to shore

Raining, hailing, wind is wailing
Hear the thunder roar!

Row row row your boat
Find a place that's dry
Scurry, scuttle, hide and huddle
Till the storm blows by.

Row row row your boat
And away you go

29

Skies are clearing, sunset nearing
Homeward bound you row.

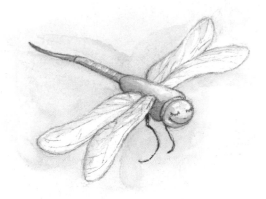

Row Row Row Your Boat

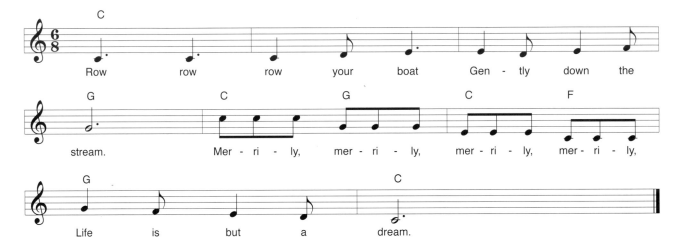

Row row row your boat Gen - tly down the stream. Mer - ri - ly, mer - ri - ly, mer - ri - ly, mer - ri - ly, Life is but a dream.

2. Row row row your boat
Happy as can be
Sunshine glowing, off and rowing
With your family.

3. Row row row your boat
Stroke and follow through
Fumbling, flailing, oars go sailing—
What a clumsy crew!

4. Row row row your boat
Row with all your might
Rocking, bashing, water splashing
Better hold on tight!

5. Row row row your boat
Look ahead to find
Beavers damming, logging, jamming
Left you in a bind!

6. Row row row your boat
Stop to have a munch
Chomping, snacking, slurping, smacking
What a noisy bunch!

7. Row row row your boat
Better row to shore
Raining, hailing, wind is wailing
Hear the thunder roar!

8. Row row row your boat
Find a place that's dry
Scurry, scuttle, hide and huddle
Till the storm blows by.

9. Row row row your boat
And away you go
Skies are clearing, sunset nearing
Homeward bound you row.

R0093094488

FEB 15 2002

~~MARTIN LUTHER KING, JR.~~

J
782.42164
TRAPANI

Trapani, Iza.

Row, row, row your boat

DISCARDED

PEACHTREE

Atlanta-Fulton Public Library